DETECTO-GRAMS
AND OTHER PUZZLES

by H. A. RIPLEY
and
F. GREGORY HARTSWICK

Bell Publishing Company
New York

CONTENTS

This 1983 edition is published by Bell Publishing Company,
distributed by Crown Publishers, Inc. by arrangement with
Liberty Library Corporation.

Manufactured in the United States of America

Library of Congress Cataloging in Publication Data

Ripley, H.A. (Harold Austin), 1896-
    Detectograms and other puzzles.

    Reprint. Originally published: New York : Scholastic Book
Services, c1968.
    Contents: Detectograms / by H.A. Ripley—Puzzles /
by F. Gregory Hartswick—Answers to detectograms—
Answers to puzzles.
    1. Puzzles.   2. Detective and mystery stories.
I. Hartswick, F. Gregory (Frederic Gregory), 1891-
II. Title.
GV1507.D4R56   1982   793.73   82-20775
ISBN: 0-517-402998

h g f e d c b a

DETECTOGRAMS   by H. A. Ripley

No. 1   So This Is London!

"The foggiest morning in London's history! That is a favorite phrase of English detective story writers." Professor Stiggins was talking to his class in criminology.

"Well, I actually encountered such a fog on my first visit to his Britannic Majesty's capital. I had an appointment on the Strand, and as vehicular transportation was out of the question I set out on foot. The fog was actually so thick one could hardly see two feet ahead. Soon I was hopelessly lost.

"I stumbled and wandered about for half an hour or so. The fog was as thick as ever. Just as I got to the middle of a block, I heard a shot fired. Walking in the direction from which the sound seemed to come, I soon found myself at a corner where a crowd was huddled about a prostrate figure.

"A bobby was soon on the job (great chaps, those London police), and I was about to go on my way when I heard someone shout, 'There he goes!'

"As a figure dashed ahead, not a foot from me, I tripped him, and after a struggle the constable slipped the cuffs on.

"I'm afraid I'll have to consider you embryo detectives quite hopeless if you can't quickly tell me what is the one thing quite wrong with my little story."

CAN YOU TELL WHAT?*

---

*Answers in back of book, page 74.

"Here is a good illustration of the old bromide that the smartest criminal leaves some clue in even the most carefully planned crime," mused Professor Stiggins.

"I was in Colshire, a beautiful little English village, at the time. I was asked by the local police to assist them in a rather puzzling affair.

"A man had been brutally murdered. Suspicion had been directed toward an illiterate underworld character who had been accused of sending the following note, found on the murdered man's desk:

> sir john when i last seen you i sed i ment bizness i will kil you if the muney aint here by mundy; all of it
>
> yurs truley,   XX

"When Wellington, the Chief Constable, asked my opinion, I told him the writer of the note, and therefore probably the murderer, was obviously an educated man. After explaining why I was sure of that, he agreed with me. The investigation took a different turn, the murderer was caught, and, as I suspected, he was an intelligent, educated man."

"Well, Professor," remarked Bill Cargo, to whom Stiggins had been speaking, "this letter doesn't appear to me to be the result of a college education."

HOW HAD THE PROFESSOR DETER-MINED THAT THE WRITER OF THE NOTE WAS AN EDUCATED MAN?

No. 3　　An Easy Combination

"I was working late, preparing an advertising campaign," said Fellows. "About ten fifteen I heard the outer office door click. Being unarmed, I hurriedly turned out the lights in my office and waited breathlessly, as there was a large sum of money in the safe. I knew my chances of attracting attention from the tenth floor were small, so reaching for the phone I hastily dialed headquarters and told them in a low voice to send help immediately. Then, creeping noiselessly to the open safe, I gently shut the door, twirled the combination, and crawled behind a big old-fashioned desk.

"In a few minutes the robber entered my office, flashed his light over the place, and went to the safe. He had it open in about two minutes, took the money, and left. That's all I know about it."

"What time is it now, Mr. Fellows?" inquired Professor Stiggins.

"Why, I haven't a watch."

"How, then, did you know it was about ten fifteen when you heard the door click?"

"I had gone for a sandwich and I left the restaurant next door at ten five. I had been back about five minutes," replied Fellows.

"You say the burglar was masked," continued the professor. "How did you know that?"

"As he put down his light to open the safe, I could see the mask," returned Fellows belligerently.

"Very interesting, Fellows," smiled the professor, "but you'll have to be a better liar than that to fool me."

WHERE DID THE PROFESSOR DETECT THE LIE?

No. 4   Too Clever

"Receiving no reply to my ring and finding the door unlocked, I went in," said Lynch. "Dawson was seated at his desk, shot through the head. Seeing he was dead, I called the police and remained here."

"Touch anything, Lynch?" asked Professor Stiggins.

"No sir, nothing."

"Positive of that, are you?"

"Absolutely, sir."

The professor made a careful examination of the desk and found Dawson had been writing a letter at the time of the tragedy. Presumably recognizing his slayer, he had managed to tear off a piece of paper and scrawl on it. "D.A. did thi—" and here it trailed off. Apparently the murderer had not seen this scrap of paper which the professor found under the letter.

Further examination disclosed several kinds of writing paper, a pen tray holding the recently used pen, inkwell, eraser, stamps, letters, and bills. The gun from which the shot had been fired was on the floor by the side of the chair, and the bullet was found embedded in the divan.

"Well," mused the professor, "this D.A. didn't see that scrawled message and he overlooked something else in his desire to make it appear suicide. Although Dawson could have shot himself, I know it was murder, and I know the murderer or someone else was in this room after that message had been written. Lynch is beyond suspicion."

"It's murder right enough," said Inspector Kelley, "but I don't see how you know someone was in this room after the message had been scrawled."

HOW DID THE PROFESSOR KNOW?

"Who shot her?" cried Rogers as he rushed into the hospital three minutes after his ex-wife died from a bullet through her head.

"Just a minute, Mr. Rogers," said Professor Stiggins. "We'll have to ask you a few questions—routine, you know. Although divorced for the past six months, you have been living in the same house with your ex-wife, have you not?"

"That's right," replied Rogers.

"Had any trouble recently?"

"Well, yesterday, when I told her I was going on a business trip, she threatened to commit suicide. In fact, I grabbed a bottle of iodine from her as she was about to drink it. When I left last evening at seven, however, telling her I was spending the night with friends in Sewickley, she made no objection. Returning to town this afternoon," continued Rogers, "I called my home and the maid answered."

"Just what did she say?" inquired Stiggins.

"'Oh, Mr. Rogers, they took poor mistress to St. Ann's Hospital 'bout half an hour ago. Please hurry to her.'

"She was crying, so I couldn't get anything else out of her; then I hurried here. Where is she?"

"The nurse will direct you," said Stiggins with a nod.

"A queer case, this, Professor," said Inspector Kelley. "These moderns are a little too much for me, I'm afraid. A man and woman living together after being divorced six months!"

"A queer case indeed, Inspector," mused the professor, "and you'd better detain Mr. Rogers. If he didn't shoot her himself, I'm confident he knows who did."

WHY DID THE PROFESSOR ADVISE THE INSPECTOR TO DETAIN ROGERS?

No. 6   A Rum Regatta

"I heard an amusing story last night," said Jud Squires to Professor Stiggins, as the two men sat in the latter's study.

"Everything amuses you," the professor remarked, "so perhaps you'd better let me judge its humor."

"Well," continued Squires, "I was talking last night with Dan Starritt. Starritt, you know, provides our elite with prohibited beverages. However, despite his so-called profession, he's a scintillating fellow.

"According to his story, three rumrunners came to him one morning in Nassau, where he is well known, seeking advice in connection with a wager they had made among themselves the night before. It seems that the three of them, having sampled too freely of the liquor they were to take the next day to Miami, had agreed to put up $3,000 which was to be the prize of the owner of the last boat to reach Miami. They forgot for the moment that their boss was in a hurry for the liquor.

"In the sober light of morning they wondered how they could reach Miami on schedule without changing their wager, which these sporting gentlemen were reluctant to do. Eventually they had come to Starritt, who solved their problem by whispering the same advice to each of them. These whispered words sent them racing to the boats and they started for Miami at top speed.

"The wager hadn't been changed any," continued Squires, "so what had Starritt whispered that caused them to race the boats in an effort to win the $3,000 prize?"

The professor was momentarily stumped, but at last he smiled and said: "Why, there's only one thing Starritt could have said."

NOW, WHAT WAS IT?

"Come in, Hayden," said Professor Stiggins. "We've finally located Jim Wilson. He's living at the Sterling, that dump down near the river. Know where it is?"

"Sure," replied Hayden. "I know it, but you can't expect any cooperation from the guy that runs the joint—I know that."

"Don't let that bother you," continued the professor. "Wilson's up against it, and he's got to get in touch with his brother Bill. We know Bill's in town, but haven't found him yet. Now, I want you to tail Jim everywhere he goes. Adams will relieve you. When he leaves the hotel, don't let him out of your sight—day or night. Eventually he'll lead you to his brother. Both you and Adams know Bill, and as the Sterling has only one entrance you shouldn't have much trouble."

"Right, sir; he won't give us the slip," said Hayden confidently as he left the office.

He was the best shadow in the department, and Adams, his relief, was almost as good.

Bill Wilson, learning his brother was staying at the Sterling and was under constant surveillance once he left the hotel, resorted to a simple ruse that enabled him to see his brother Jim at the hotel unmolested.

WHAT RUSE DID BILL USE?

No. 8   A Question of Identity

Professor Stiggins and three of his friends were enjoying their weekly "get together" at the University Club.

"Professor," said Patrie, "tell us something about that Yelpir murder case you were working on."

"Well, gentlemen," said the professor in his retiring manner, "as you know, Yelpir's affairs were common knowledge, and the fact that several women had reasons to wish him dead complicated matters a bit.

"His body was found in his study, which opened on to a corridor. At the other end of the corridor and directly opposite it a staircase led to the servants' quarters above.

"Diana Lane, a house guest of Mrs. Yelpir at the time of the murder, was questioned, and she appeared nervous. She insisted, however, that she had been in her room at the time Yelpir was slain.

"Nora, a servant, testified that as she was descending the stairs leading from the servants' quarters she saw Diana Lane, wearing her famous emerald pendant and dressed in an enticing black negligee, walk down the lighted corridor to Yelpir's room. Shocked at seeing Yelpir open the door to Diana, Nora fled back to her room. When questioned regarding her presence in the corridor, Nora explained that she had been on her way to the pantry for a sandwich.

"In the face of such evidence Miss Lane admitted having gone to the study at the time.

"While Miss Lane's reputation wasn't above reproach," concluded the professor, "I knew without further investigation that Nora's testimony was maliciously false"

FROM THIS EVIDENCE, HOW DID THE PROFESSOR KNOW THAT NORA WAS FALSELY TRYING TO INCRIMINATE DIANA LANE?

"I've often remarked," said Professor Stiggins, in an expansive mood, "how very difficult it is to fake an alibi without someone's assistance. A case in point is a messy affair we cleared up recently.

"I wasn't definitely suspicious of Picus when I happened to bump into him the morning after an acquaintance of his had been found dead under suspicious circumstances. I rather casually asked him where he had been and what he had been doing the previous afternoon about four o'clock, the apparent time of the man's death. He related the following story:

"'As it was a beautiful day yesterday, I took my sailboat out about noon. About three o'clock, however, when I was perhaps fifteen miles out, the wind died down completely. There wasn't a breath of air, and I knew that unless I could attract some boat I was in for an uncomfortable time. Remembering that the international distress signal is a flag flown upside down, I ran mine up the mast in that manner.

"'In about an hour the steamer *Leone* hove to, and I went aboard her after securing my boat with a towline. The captain said he had seen my distress signal through his binoculars and would put me ashore at the first convenient place. He did so, and a passing motorist gave me a lift back

18

to town. Imagine my surprise when I read in the paper this morning that the *Leone* had been sunk in a storm after putting me ashore, and all hands had been lost!'

"While I knew," remarked the professor, "that the *Leone* had been sunk with all on board, after hearing Picus' story I immediately arrested him on suspicion of murder."

WHAT WAS WRONG WITH PICUS' ALIBI?

Inspector Kelley and Professor Stiggins were seated in the former's office when Policeman Fanning and his charge entered. After Fanning's hurried explanation, Jasper told his story:

"I'm the ticket taker on a merry-go-round at Coney Island. This bein' Saturday, we had a big crowd. The trip was almost over when I reached out saying, 'Ticket, please,' and I see this woman sittin' up in the middle of the chariot with that terrible look on her face. She didn't answer, and when I shook her she slumped over in the corner. I screamed, jumped off, and ran for the manager. I got this blood on my hand when I shook her.

"Yes, sir, she'd ridden before — a couple of times — and I seen the man she was with on the two rides before. He jumped off just before I got to her. Just happened to see him."

"The doctor said she had been stabbed through the heart and died instantly?" Professor Stiggins asked the policeman.

"That's right, sir."

"It seems strange, Jasper," remarked the professor, "that you can give such a good description of this woman's companion on two previous rides when you just 'happened' to notice him jump off. Does the merry-go-round ever make you dizzy?"

"No, sir, I'm used to it."

"Well, Inspector," said the professor, turning to his friend, "I suppose you are going to hold this man?"

"Certainly," replied Kelley. "That's just about the weakest story of a murder I've ever heard."

WHAT JUSTIFIED THE POLICE IN HOLDING JASPER?

One of Professor Stiggins' eccentricities is his flat refusal to write reports. He even conducts his social correspondence by telegraph. Sometimes this is a bit trying on his associates, as he delights in making his telegraphs somewhat baffling, although perfectly clear. Here are some of his telegraphic reports. In them is every fact and clue necessary for a solution—and each has only one possible answer.

E F CAVANAUGH   APRIL 22 1933
   STATES ATTORNEYS INVESTIGATOR
      PEORIA ILLINOIS
CHADWICK SAYS WHILE COMING UP DRIVE
SAW MAN CLIMB LADDER OPEN WINDOW
AND ENTER HIS BEDROOM STOP THAT HE
HURRIED AS QUICKLY AS HIS LAMENESS
ALLOWED TO HOUSE WHICH WAS SECURELY
LOCKED STOP GOT PISTOL FROM LIBRARY
QUIETLY PHONED POLICE THEN WENT UP-
STAIRS TO FIND BURGLAR HAD ALREADY
ESCAPED WITH VALUABLE JEWELRY FROM
DRESSER STOP ON FLOOR TO LEFT OF
ROPE LADDER HOOKED TO INSIDE SILL I
DISCOVERED WOMANS THREE CARAT DIA-
MOND RING STOP FOUND INDISTINCT FOOT-
PRINTS ON WINDOWSILL AND DRIED MUD
ON RUG STOP CHADWICK SAYS STRONG

EAST WIND BLOWING AT TIME STOP FROM
ABOVE YOU WILL SEE ROBBERY WAS FAKED
STABUS STIGGINS

Why was Stiggins confident Chadwick had
faked the robbery?

No. 12

APRIL 29 1933

LIEUTENANT ANDREW J HUDOCK
PENNSYLVANIA STATE POLICE
HERSEY PENNSYLVANIA

MADAM DUPONT ALONE WITH NURSE IN FORMERS BEDROOM LAST NIGHT STOP NURSE SAID MADAM WHILE UNDRESSING FLUNG CLOTHES IN HEAP ON CHAIR SUDDENLY BECAME INSANE GRABBED KNIFE FROM TRAY AND CUT THROAT BEFORE SHE COULD INTERVENE STOP DRESS LYING TOP OF PILE BORE FOUR DARK STAINS AND SMALL SLASH ACROSS BOSOM STOP MAKING ULTRAVIOLET EXAMINATION TOMORROW STOP NURSE SAYS SHE DISTURBED NOTHING IN ROOM BEFORE MY ARRIVAL STOP FOUND BODY LYING CENTER OF BED BLOODY KNIFE ON FLOOR BENEATH OUTFLUNG HAND STOP MIDDLE FINGERTIP BRUISED STOP HAVING ABOVE CLUE TO TRAGEDY AM WAITING STOP CONFIDENT NURSE WILL FURTHER INCRIMINATE SELF
STABUS STIGGINS

Why was Stiggins certain of the nurse's guilt?

GEORGE VICTOR GAVAZA   APRIL 15 1933
  PRESIDENT SIPHO PRODUCTS CORPORA-
           TION
   BOSTON MASSACHUSETTS
JOE WILKINS ONLY ONE WHO KNEW LOCA-
TION OF GENUINE BURIED TREASURE STOP
AT 3 PM YESTERDAY MAP MARKING LOCA-
TION OF IT MIDWAY BETWEEN TWO BOUL-
DERS ON DESERT NINE MILES FROM HERE
STOLEN FROM HIM STOP REALIZING IM-
POSSIBILITY OF RECOVERING TREASURE
ALONE BEFORE DARK AND CERTAINTY THAT
THIEVES WOULD DO SO AT NIGHT APPEALED
TO ME STOP WITHOUT TOUCHING TREA-
SURE WE HAD PLEASURE OF OBSERVING
THIEVES WHO CLOSELY FOLLOWED MAP
LEAVE VICINITY EMPTY HANDED AFTER
MUCH FUTILE DIGGING STOP WE RE-
COVERED TREASURE TODAY AND SENDING
JOE TO YOU FOR FINANCIAL ADVICE STOP
IF YOU WANT HIS CONFIDENCE BETTER
FIGURE RUSE WE EMPLOYED TO OUTWIT
THIEVES   STABUS STIGGINS

How did Stiggins, without touching it, save
Joe's treasure?

No. 14

APRIL 1 1933

EX DEPUTY SHERIFF HARRY BECKMAN
TULSA OKLAHOMA
REPORT ON STINSON CASE STOP SIX MONTHS AGO STINSON MADE WILL LEAVING LARGE ESTATE TO STEPDAUGHTER GRACE STOP TODAY INFORMED HER HE WAS RUINED FINANCIALLY STOP SHE SAYS AFTER ASSURING HIM IT MADE NO DIFFERENCE SHE STARTED LEAVE ROOM WHEN STINSON TOOK PISTOL AND BLEW OUT BRAINS STOP GRACE SAYS RUSHED TO PHONE AND CALLED POLICE THEN FAINTED STOP I FOUND STINSON SEATED AT LIBRARY DESK HEAD RESTING ON OUTSTRETCHED ARMS BLOOD COAGULATED AROUND TEMPLE WOUND STOP IN FAINTING GRACE APPARENTLY PULLED PHONE TO FLOOR STOP FOUND HER LYING ON PISTOL BESIDE STINSONS CHAIR STOP THEY WERE ALONE STOP FINGERPRINTS ON GUN SMEARED STOP HOLDING HER FOR MURDER

STABUS STIGGINS

Do you know why?

FEBRUARY 11 1933
WALTER B PRESTON PRESIDENT
UNIVERSAL FIRE INSURANCE COMPANY
NEW YORK NEW YORK
RECEIVED YOUR TELEGRAM STATING THAT
BECAUSE OF LARGE AMOUNT FIRE INSUR-
ANCE RECENTLY TAKEN OUT BY STERLING
MANUFACTURING COMPANY YOU WERE
SUSPICIOUS THAT THEIR CLAIM AGAINST
YOU FOR SIX THOUSAND MENS SUITS
FRAUDULENT STOP I IMMEDIATELY INVESTI-
GATED STOP FOUND NO INDICATION OF
INCENDIARY ORIGIN OF FIRE BUT THERE
WERE CERTAIN OTHER SUSPICIOUS CIR-
CUMSTANCES STOP DISCOVERED NOTHING
DEFINITE UNTIL I INSPECTED ROOM WHERE
SUITS WERE SUPPOSEDLY STOCKED STOP
ALTHOUGH FOUND LARGE QUANTITY BADLY
CHARRED MENS SUIT MATERIAL IT IS
WHAT I DID NOT FIND THAT CONCLUSIVELY
PROVES FRAUD STOP JOHN BROOKS PRESI-
DENT BEGS YOU NOT TO PROSECUTE AD-
VISE   STABUS STIGGINS

What did Stiggins fail to find?

No. 16

LEONARDE - KEELER FORENSIC
PSYCHOLOGIST
SCIENTIFIC CRIME DETECTION
LABORATORY
CHICAGO ILLINOIS
WEALTHY HAROLD GIFFORD DISCOVERED
THIS MORNING ON HIS LIBRARY FLOOR
SHOT THROUGH HEART STOP THREE MEN
JOHNSON JONES AND JEFFRIES WHO ARE
THIEF BLACKMAILER AND MURDERER BUT
NOT RESPECTIVELY KNOWN TO HAVE
VISITED HIM LAST NIGHT STOP JONES AD-
MITS BLACKMAILING GIFFORD STOP JOHN-
SONS GOLF SCORE CONSISTENTLY BELOW
ONE HUNDRED STOP JEFFRIES HAD MEA-
SLES WHEN HE WAS FOUR YEARS OLD STOP
HAVE ARRESTED GIFFORDS MURDERER
STOP WHAT IS HIS NAME   STIGGIE

It is one of the three. Which one?

                              FEBRUARY 25 1933
CHIEF INSPECTOR MORAN
   POLICE HEADQUARTERS
   NEW YORK NEW YORK
REPORT ON HALLOWEEN ROADHOUSE TRAG-
EDY STOP THREE COUPLES TOOK PRIVATE
DINING ROOM AT ONE OCLOCK STOP WOM-
EN COSTUMED AS FOLLOWS RUSSIAN PEAS-
ANT MARTHA WASHINGTON AND JULIET MEN
GREEK PHILOSOPHER ROBIN HOOD AND
CAPUCHIN MONK STOP SUPPER SERVED BY
WAITER WHO FAILED TO OBSERVE SEATING
ARRANGEMENT STOP HOUR LATER SHRIEK
HEARD AND FIVE RAN OUT LEAVING JULIET
DEAD FROM QUICK ACTING POISON STOP
SUICIDE RULED OUT STOP SUSPICIOUS CIR-
CUMSTANCE IS ENTIRE ABSENCE FINGER-
PRINTS AT PLACE NEAREST DEAD WOMAN
STOP ALTHOUGH POSITIVELY NOTHING
FOUND BELONGING TO HIM OR HIS COS-
TUME KNOW THAT ROBIN HOOD SAT AT
THAT PLACE SO CONCENTRATE HUNT ON
HIM   STABUS STIGGINS

How did Stiggins know that Robin Hood had
sat at that particular place?

JANUARY 7 1933

CHIEF INSPECTOR MORAN
  POLICE HEADQUARTERS
  NEW YORK NEW YORK
REGARDING BLACK CASE STOP HIS LABORA-
TORY LOCKED AND BOLTED AND AS WIN-
DOWS AFFORDED NO MEANS OF ENTRANCE
BROKE IN DOOR AND DISCOVERED BLACK
DEAD FROM TWO BULLET WOUNDS THRU
HEAD WITH 32 CALIBER AUTOMATIC BEAR-
ING ONLY HIS FINGERPRINTS BESIDE BODY
STOP LETTER IN HIS POCKET SIGNED BY
NOTORIOUS GANGSTER CASSIDY THREAT-
ENING TO KILL BLACK UNLESS HE PAID
CASSIDY MONEY CASSIDY CLAIMED OWED
ON SHADY DEAL STOP FOUND CIGARETTE
STUB ON FLOOR BUT NO BURNED MATCHES
STOP NO LIGHTER ON BLACK STOP CASSIDY
ADMITS WRITING LETTER BUT DISCLAIMS
ANY KNOWLEDGE OF DEATH AND WHILE HIS
ALIBI WEAK WE CAN NEVER PIN THIS ON
CASSIDY SO RELEASED HIM

STABUS STIGGINS

How did Stiggins know that Cassidy was innocent?

No. 19

CHIEF OF POLICE JOHN DAWSON
POLICE HEADQUARTERS
PORTLAND MAINE
SCENE OF LOOMIS TRAGEDY OLD COLONIAL
MANSION WITH SOFT GREEN CARPETING
THROUGHOUT SETTING OFF PRICELESS
STATUARY AND ANTIQUE FURNITURE TO
BEST ADVANTAGE STOP WINTON LOOMIS
SAYS WAS SAILING WHEN FORCED ASHORE
MILE AWAY BY STORM THAT HE WALKED
HOME AND UPON ENTERING FRONT DOOR
HEARD SHOT BUT COULDNT LOCATE IT BE-
CAUSE OF THUNDER AND THAT AFTER IN-
VESTIGATING THREE FRONT ROOMS DIS-
COVERED HIS WIFE IN STUDIO AT REAR
SHOT DEAD STOP CLAIMS TOUCHED NOTH-
ING STOP ALL WINDOWS IN STUDIO CLOSED
BUT DRAPES AT ONE RAINSOAKED STOP
BELIEVE LOOMIS CAUGHT IN STORM ALL
RIGHT AS FOUND HIS MUD TRACKS NEAR
WIFES BODY BUT YOU UNDERSTAND WHY
AM BRINGING HIM IN   STABUS STIGGINS

Why did Stiggins arrest Loomis?

No. 20

DISTRICT ATTORNEY ROBERT J HALL
   CRIMINAL COURTS BUILDING
      CHICAGO ILLINOIS
MEDICAL EXAMINER JUST COMPLETED AU-
TOPSY ON CHARRED BODY OF LUCILLE
GOODSPEED WHICH DISCLOSED CAUSE OF
DEATH WAS KNIFE WOUND NEAR HEART
AND NOT FIRE AS FIRST BELIEVED WHEN I
WAS INFORMED POLICE HAD INTERCEPTED
ANONYMOUS BLACKMAILING LETTER TO
HER SWEETHEART WEALTHY ROGER WIL-
TERDING STATING WRITER KNEW HE HAD
STABBED LUCILLE AND WOULD INFORM
POLICE UNLESS WILTERDING LEFT FIVE
THOUSAND DOLLARS AT DESIGNATED SPOT
STOP WILTERDING RECEIVED LETTER WITH-
OUT KNOWLEDGE OF ITS INTERCEPTION
AND WHEN HE GOT SIMILAR LETTER AGAIN
YESTERDAY AND REPORTED NEITHER TO
POLICE THEY ARRESTED HIM DESPITE HIS
UNQUESTIONABLE ALIBI STOP YOULL SEE
WHERE MURDERER REALLY SLIPPED
                    STABUS STIGGINS

Can you see where the murderer slipped?

No. 21

JOSEPH A KAVANAGH   JANUARY 28 1933
    INTERNATIONAL SECRET SERVICE
        INSTITUTE
    HOBOKEN NEW JERSEY

HER COOK CLAIMS FOUND MRS NORMAN BROOKS BRUTALLY STABBED TO DEATH STOP MADE FOLLOWING STATEMENT THEN FAINTED QUOTE THIS WAS MY AFTERNOON OFF AND AS I THINK CLARK GABLE WONDERFUL WENT SEE HIM IN A FREE SOUL THEN I WENT SHOPPING TOOK A WALK IN THE PARK AND RETURNED TO FIND MY POOR MISTRESS MURDERED SHE WAS SO GOOD AND KIND TOO UNQUOTE ONE WOUND WENT CLEAR THROUGH NECK STOP APPARENTLY BUTCHER KNIFE USED STOP WHEN INSPECTOR WATERS INFORMED OF ABOVE STATED MRS BROOKS UNDOUBTEDLY MURDERED BY A MAN SO COULDNT UNDERSTAND WHY I ARRESTED COOK STOP CAN YOU   STABUS STIGGINS

Why did Stiggins arrest the cook?

MARCH 11 1933
SUPERINTENDENT OF POLICE JOHN J FAHEY
  BALTIMORE MARYLAND
COLONEL WICKERSHAM AND MYSELF AT-
TENDING CLASS REUNION AT UNIVERSITY
STOP WHILE WALKING IN DORMITORY GAR-
DEN TONIGHT STUMBLED ACROSS ROGERS
BODY LYING DIRECTLY BELOW HIS SIXTH
FLOOR WINDOW STOP WICKERSHAM JOINED
ME EXPLAINING HE HAD GONE TO ROGERS
ROOM FOR MATCH FINDING IT EMPTY AND
SUICIDE NOTE ON DRESSER OPENED WIN-
DOW AND SEEING SOMEONE BELOW CAME
DOWN STOP FIFTEEN MINUTES LATER ROG-
ERS ROOMMATE WATSON RETURNED DE-
CLARING HE HAD GONE DRUGSTORE FOR
MEDICINE ALSO THAT ROGERS HAD THREAT-
ENED SUICIDE STOP INVESTIGATIONS ES-
TABLISH NO ONE IN ROOM BEFORE TRAGEDY
BUT ROGERS AND WATSON STOP WICKER-
SHAM BEYOND SUSPICION STOP HOLDING
WATSON FOR MURDER   STABUS STIGGINS

How did Stiggins conclude that Watson is the
murderer?

No. 23

MARCH 18 1933

COLONEL CALVIN GODDARD
SCIENTIFIC CRIME DETECTION
LABORATORY
CHICAGO ILLINOIS

FOUND DORSEY OWINGS BAREFOOTED AND CLAD IN PAJAMAS LYING ON LEFT ARM AGAINST BATHROOM WALL DEAD FROM INSTANTLY FATAL BULLET WOUND IN RIGHT TEMPLE STOP 38 CALIBER AUTOMATIC BEARING UNIDENTIFIABLE FINGERPRINTS ON FLOOR NEAR HIP STOP NO BLOOD INSIDE OF EJECTED SHELL LYING FOUR FEET FROM GUN WHICH WAS BY OUTSTRETCHED HAND CLUTCHING UNSIGNED NOTE IN FEMININE WRITING PROCLAIMING UNDYING LOVE STOP OWINGS AND WIFE SYBIL ALONE AT TIME OF TRAGEDY STOP SHE CLAIMS THAT ON HER REFUSAL GRANT HUSBAND DIVORCE HE KILLED HIMSELF WHILE SHE WAS IN BEDROOM STOP OWINGS SLIPPERS FOUND IN BATHTUB STOP HOLDING SYBIL FOR MURDER   STABUS STIGGINS

Do you know why?

No. 24

FEBRUARY 18 1933

STATES ATTORNEY GEORGE A TRACY
CITY HALL
PHILADELPHIA PENNSYLVANIA

CLARA EVANS COAT AND HAT WASHED ASHORE AT BRENT BOATHOUSE STOP ALTHOUGH HER BODY RECOVERED WITH GRAPPLING HOOKS BORE BRUISES ON BACK OF HEAD AND LEFT SIDE DROWNING CAUSE OF DEATH STOP ALLEN STATES THEY WERE IN MIDDLE OF RIVER OPPOSITE BRENTS WHEN TWO MOTOR BOATS SPED BY CAUSING HEAVY WASH AT WHICH CLARA BECAME FRIGHTENED AND IN EXCITEMENT CAPSIZED CANOE STOP CURRENT STRONG THERE AND AS NIGHT VERY DARK ALLEN CLAIMS COULDNT LOCATE HER STOP EXPLAINS TWO HOUR DELAY IN REPORTING TRAGEDY BY STATEMENT HE WAS PRACTICALLY UNCONSCIOUS WHEN HE MADE SHORE STOP HES LYING SO AM DETAINING HIM   STABUS STIGGINS

Why was Stiggins justified?

No. 25

LIEUT W C GORDON   MARCH 25 1933
  BUREAU OF IDENTIFICATION
    KANSAS CITY KANSAS
AM HOLDING WINTERS BRONSON RAN-
DOLPH AND HUDSON IN KIDNAPPING OF
FOSTER BABY AND HAVE LEARNED FOLLOW-
ING FACTS STOP ONE OF FOUR KILLED
BABYS NURSE STOP GANG LEADER AND
KILLER ALMOST DOUBLES IN APPEARANCE
STOP HUDSON AND KILLER WITHOUT LEAD-
ERS KNOWLEDGE HAD RECENTLY ATTEMPT-
ED ANOTHER KIDNAPING WHICH FELL THRU
STOP BRONSON AND LEADER ARRANGED
GETAWAY AND HIDEOUT STOP WINTERS
AND KILLER HAD BOTH INSISTED LEADER
PERSONALLY PICK UP RANSOM MONEY
STOP LEADER AND KILLER ARE BOTH COUS-
INS OF RANDOLPH STOP YOU WILL SEE
FROM ABOVE WHO IS KILLER AND WHO IS
LEADER   STABUS STIGGINS

Who is killer and who is leader of gang?

No. 26

   CHIEF OF POLICE
      HINSDALE ILLINOIS
FOUND JAMISON IN CHAIR DEAD FROM
GUNSHOT WOUND AND RINKER LYING ON
FLOOR SHOT THROUGH HAND NEAR DESK
COVERED WITH SPOTLESS AND ALMOST
COMPLETED BLUEPRINT STOP RINKER SAYS
JAMISON WAS WORKING ON IMPORTANT
DRAWING AND HE WAS FINISHING BLUE-
PRINT WHEN MASKED MAN ENTERED COV-
ERED BOTH AND AS HE RINKER GRABBED
REVOLVER BANDIT SHOT JAMISON DEAD
AND ORDERED RINKER DROP GUN ON HIS
DESK AND LIE ON FLOOR STOP HE OBEYED
BUT AS GUNMAN WENT TO SAFE RINKER
RAISED HIMSELF GRABBED HIS GUN AS
BANDIT SHOT HIM STOP SAYS HE AGAIN
GRABBED GUN BUT BANDIT KNOCKED HIM
UNCONSCIOUS STOP HOLDING RINKER FOR
JAMISONS MURDER   STABUS STIGGINS

Would you have done so? Why?

Puzzles by F. Gregory Hartswick

No. 1 The Bookworm's Journey

A collector had a rare set of books in three volumes, which stood on his shelf as shown in our illustration.

One day he found that a bookworm had bored a hole straight from the first page of Volume I to the last page of Volume III. Now, the covers of the books were each one eighth of an inch thick, and the paper in each book was exactly three inches in thickness. The question is, how far did the worm travel? No, no, you're quite wrong! And there isn't any trick about the length of the worm, either. It's a perfectly straight question with a perfectly straight answer.

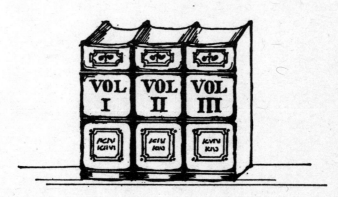

No. 2   A One-Word Puzzle

Here's an interesting little problem involving letters. Take the letters

OREDWNO

and make one word out of them.

When you have succeeded in doing this, try making one word out of the letters

ABENOTY

This last problem is said to have stumped Queen Victoria when it was given to her. In any case, not many people solve it. Still, perhaps you're one of the clever ones.

No. 3   The Fly and the Bicycles

Once upon a time there was a stretch of road twenty miles long. At each end of this road was a bicyclist, and at exactly the same instant, they started riding toward each other at a constant speed of ten miles an hour, continuing until their front wheels touched. At the instant of their starting, a fly, which was perched on the front wheel of one of the bicycles, started to fly toward the other at a speed of fifteen miles an hour. He flew until he touched the other front wheel and instantly started back, always at the same speed, till he touched the front wheel of the first, and so on, flying back and forth between the wheels until he was crushed as they met. Each journey naturally was shorter than the one before.

Now all you have to do is to figure out—exactly how far did the fly fly?

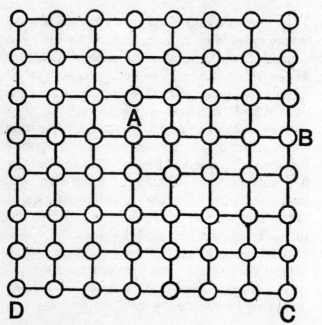

The circles shown above represent sixty-four towns. A motorist started from the town marked A and made a tour which enabled him to visit each of the other towns once, and only once, returning to his original starting place without making any diagonal trips—moving only along the roads indicated by the connecting lines. See if you can trace his route in the fewest possible STRAIGHT moves. You might start, for instance, by going from A to B—one move; then to C—

two moves; then to D—three moves; and so on. You will find this a fascinating puzzle to work on as you develop possibilities of making fewer and fewer straight journeys each time you try it. Remember, all towns must be visited, and no town can be visited more than once.

No. 5   Word-Enigma Puzzle

The answer to this puzzle is a well known quotation from Shakespeare which contains sixty-five letters. Guess the words defined below, and put the letters of each word in the positions designated by the numbers; when you have finished you will have completed the quotation. For instance, if a word was defined like this, "6-24-19-11—Organs of hearing," you would guess the word to be EARS, and put E for the 6th, A for the 24th, R for the 19th, and S for the 11th letters of the answer.

29-4-5-41-32-58-25—Imaginary line around the middle of the earth.

8-13-36-15-35-63-47—Grow better in health or quality.

18-59-37-11-34-43-53-65-16-38—Weight, consequence, value, significance.

24-2-45-23-19-62-50-10—District in northern Greece.

56-7-17—To go through the air.

1-44-27-52-49-3-14-55-9-40—Ordinal form of the unlucky number.

57-64-42-54-46-28-6-39-31-21-48—Act of voluntarily leaving office.

30-51-26-22-60—Cessation of life.

12-61-20-33—Ward off.

No. 6   The Sliding Letters Puzzle

```
I N A __ __ __ __ __ __
__ I N A __ __ __ __ __
__ __ I N A __ __ __ __
__ __ __ I N A __ __ __
__ __ __ __ I N A __ __
__ __ __ __ __ I N A __
__ __ __ __ __ __ I N A __
__ __ __ __ __ __ I N A
```

Fill the blanks above with letters so as to make words, each of which will have INA in the position indicated.

No. 7   Letter-Addition Puzzle

Starting with the one-letter word I, we add **T** and get IT. Then we add **E** and get—what? See if you can add the letters shown below (not necessarily in same order), and get a good English word each time. (No proper names allowed.)

```
I
I  T                IT
I  T  E             ?
__ __ __ R  ?
__ __ __ __ N  ?
__ __ __ __ __ A  ?
__ __ __ __ __ __ C  ?
__ __ __ __ __ __ __ O  ?
__ __ __ __ __ __ __ __ M  ?
__ __ __ __ __ __ __ __ __ P  ?
```

No. 8   Wine and Water

The following little puzzle, if properly attacked, is simple. But here is the problem:

A man has two bottles, one of which contains a pint of wine and the other a pint of water. He fills a glass from the bottle of wine and pours it into the bottle of water. Then he fills the same glass with the mixture in the water bottle and pours it into the wine bottle.

Now the question is—did he take more wine from the wine bottle than water from the water bottle? Or was it the other way around? Or was it—well, what was it?

No. 9   Links and Links

The following little puzzle, if properly attacked, is simple. Here it is:

Two men went a-tilting at the rings on a merry-go-round and each captured a certain number. Adolphus Brown beat Augustus Jones by six rings. Both winner and loser had the rings they had captured made into a chain as a souvenir of the occasion. Brown's chain was exactly sixteen inches long and Jones' a modest six inches.

The rings were all of exactly the same size and made of iron one half an inch thick. Can you tell from these statistics how many rings each man won?

No. 10   Ringing the Changes

Everybody knows the famous rhyme:
    A SUTLER sat in his ULSTER gray,
    Watching the moonbeams' LUSTRE play.
In the following verse eight words are formed
by using the same six letters. Fill the blanks with
words of the same six letters.

Four _____ labored in an abbey grand;
Not one was ever _____ the task in hand.
The first in open air pursued his toil:
A _____ he, who turned the fruitful soil.
The next, a smith, repaired a broken wheel;
With skillful hands he _____ the shrieking
    steel.
The third, a teacher, on his pupils pounced
When Greek they wrongly _____ or mispro-
    nounced.
The last his quilt _____; his needle plies;
Remains his _____ to patch, and, ere he lies
Upon his cheerless bunk, its tattered _____
    to mend;
And thus his daily chores and this my
    tale to end.

No. 11   The Flock of Ducks

The following little puzzle, if properly attacked, is simple. But here is the problem:

A man took a flock of ducks to market, and when he got back, his wife asked how he had made out. He said:

"Well, first I sold Mr. Smith half of the flock and half a duck; then I sold Mr. Brown a third of what was left and a third of a duck; then I met Mr. Robinson and talked him into taking a fourth of what was left and three fourths of a duck; and on the way home I met old man Jones and sold him a fifth of what was left and gave him a fifth of a duck for good measure. I had nineteen ducks left that I couldn't sell. There they are."

The question is how many ducks did that ingenious man take to market? It may be pointed out that no duck was divided.

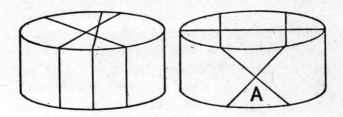

Everybody knows how to cut a plane figure into the greatest number of pieces with a given number of straight cuts—all you have to do is to be sure that each cut crosses every other cut. It was the Sam Loyd of the '90's who first investigated the matter of cutting a solid figure. He used a cheese as a sample on which to work. If you look at the two pictures above, you will see that in Fig. 1 the cheese has been cut into seven pieces with three straight cuts. And yet if you make the three cuts as in Fig. 2 you can easily see that you have gained a piece; there are seven pieces that you can see, and another on the far side, corresponding to the piece marked A.

Now into how many pieces can you cut such a cheese with four straight cuts?

No. 13   A Puzzle by Candlelight

It seems there was a man who had to work
late at the office. It seems also that the electric
lights went out, so he asked a clerk to bring him
some candles. The clerk obliged with two, each
of the same length, but, he explained as he
lighted them, one would burn for four hours and
the other for five hours. Our late-working man
finished his job and started home, but as he blew
out the candles he noticed that one was exactly
four times as long as the other. Now, he had
to charge the office for overtime, and he had
forgotten to look at his watch; however, from
the remaining lengths of the candles he was
able to figure out exactly how long he had been
working. How long a time was it?

No. 14   An Election Day Puzzle

Last election a certain William Smith was running for Commissioner on the Republican ticket, Elisha Robinson on the Share-the-Wealth, George Brown on the Demopublican, and Rufus Detwiler on the newly formed Down-with-Everything ticket. When the smoke cleared away, it was found that Mr. Smith was elected. Out of 1,648 votes cast he had received a plurality of 8 over Mr. Brown, 76 over Mr. Robinson, and 184 over Mr. Detwiler. The puzzle is to find how many votes each candidate received. It can be done almost immediately and should be done without using pencil and paper.

There is another puzzle involved in this question: What is the difference between a plurality and a majority? How many know it?

Everyone remembers the little puzzle about the missionaries, the cannibals, and the boat that would hold only two people. Here is a teaser along the same lines.

There was a treasure concealed in a lofty cell in an ancient castle. Three people—a man, a youth, and a small boy—set out one dark night to steal it. The only means of exit from the treasure room was a high window, outside which was a pulley over which was a rope with a basket at both ends. When one basket was on the ground the other was at the window. We may as well state at once, to prevent quibbling, that when a person was in the basket he could neither help himself nor be helped by anybody else. Unless there was a counterbalancing weight, he would fall freely and fatally to the ground.

Now the man weighed 195 pounds, the youth 105 pounds, the boy 90 pounds, and the box of treasure 75 pounds. It was known that the weight in the descending basket could not exceed that in the ascending basket by more than 15 pounds or the speed of descent would be so great as to injure a human being, though of course it would have no effect on the treasure. Moreover, only two persons, or one person and the treasure, could be in one basket at the same time.

The three thieves made their way to the treasure room, but could escape from it only by the basket. (Don't ask how come—this is a puzzle.) How did they make their escape, unharmed, with the loot?

No. 16   Par Golf

This puzzle is really a variation on a very old problem of measurement, and the only reason it is given a golfing twist is because there happens to be nine numbers involved, corresponding to the first nine holes of the standard golf course. It will appear that anyone who could play as required by the conditions would make Arnold Palmer look like the rankest duffer, but then, anything goes in a puzzle.

The nine holes on a golf course measure the following distances: 300 yards, 250, 200, 325, 275, 350, 225, 375, and 400. Now we assume that a player can always hit his ball exactly one of two distances in a perfectly straight line, so that it will either go toward the hole, pass over it, or drop into it (that is why such a player would completely destroy Arnold Palmer at his best). Making such an assumption, what two distances would you choose to go the first nine holes in the fewest number of strokes? If you select 125 and 75 yards, for instance, you can get around in 28 strokes. You would take four 75-yard shots for No. 1, two 125-yard shots for No. 2, one 125-yard shot and one 75-yard shot for No. 3, and so on. But those two distances are not the best you can select. Can you find the two distances that will give you the fewest number of strokes for the nine holes?

No. 17   A Little Pure Reason

The following puzzles require only the exercise of the reasoning faculties; you may discard pencil, paper, and what you remember of your arithmetic. Here is the first:

Two planes start simultaneously from San Francisco and New York, each bound on a non-stop flight across the continent. In round figures it is 2,500 miles between the cities. Each plane has a cruising speed of 250 miles an hour, and carries enough gasoline for ten hours. Which plane crashed, and why?

The second puzzle is as follows: Three men entered a hotel washroom at the same time. Two of them have black smudges on their faces. They look at each other, and all three burst out laughing. Almost immediately one of the smudged pair realizes his plight and goes to wash his face. How did this man reason that he was marked? No mirrors allowed; the conclusion is reached by logic.

No. 18   The Captive Princess

Once upon a time a knight set out to ride to the castle of a beautiful princess. For his own personal reasons, it was essential that he get there at exactly five o'clock. Now this knight was good at mathematics, and he figured that if he rode at the rate of fifteen miles an hour he would arrive one hour too soon; while if he rode at the rate of ten miles an hour he would get there one hour too late.

From these statistics can you tell (a) when this knight started his journey, (b) how far he had to ride, and (c) at what rate of speed he rode?

No. 19   Nine Tricky Dots

•   •   •

•   •   •

•   •   •

Above is shown an arrangement of nine dots in a square or rectangle. The arrangement is simple enough; so is the statement of the puzzle, which is this: Start anywhere you like and draw a continuous line which shall pass through all of the dots, making only three turnings.

Another way of putting it is to say, "Draw four straight lines which shall pass through all the dots without taking your pencil off the paper." Suppose you started at the lower left-hand corner and drew a line to the upper left-hand corner and then proceeded diagonally to the lower right-hand corner; you would have made one turning, or two straight lines.

Those are the conditions. Simple, as we said. The solution? Well, possibly just as simple; possibly not. . . . Oh, by the way, no tricks, like using two pencils at once, or folding the paper. This puzzle is strictly on the up-and-up. It can be done.

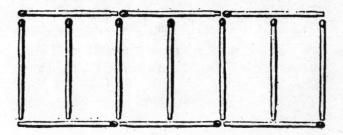

Above we show thirteen matches so arranged
that they enclose six spaces all of the same size.
These matches represent sections of fence and
were arranged as shown by a farmer who wanted
six equal-sized pens for his sheep. One night a
miscreant removed one of the fence sections
and rearranged the twelve that were left so that
they still enclosed six pens of equal size. How
did he do it? All the twelve matches must be
fairly used, with no doubles or loose ends.

No. 21   Airplane Racing

A recent airplane race was held around a circular course. While watching the death-defying speed of the pilots, a spectator remarked, "I hope young Jimmy Tailspin wins! He's the handsomest thing!"

We might make a puzzle by asking our readers what was the sex of the spectator who spoke the above words, but let us proceed.

Another spectator said, "Which one is he?"

"He's the one in the plane that has red fuselage and silver wings."

"Oh, yes," replied the second spectator. "There he goes now. By the way, how many planes are there in this race?"

The reply of the first spectator was perhaps not in character, but here it is:

"A third of the number of planes in front of him added to three quarters of the number of planes behind him will give you the answer."

So how many planes were there in the race?

No. 22   Painting the Lampposts

During a recent wave of civic improvement a contract was let to two men to paint the lampposts along a certain street. It happened that there was the same number of posts on each side of the street, and the contract was let accordingly—one man to paint the posts on the east side, the other to take care of those on the west side.

Mike, who was an early riser, arrived on the scene first and had painted three posts on the east side before Pat arrived. Pat immediately pointed out that Mike's contract called for the west side, not the east. Mike thereupon started over again on the west, while Pat went on with the work on the east. When Pat had finished his side he went across the street and painted six posts for Mike. (It is obvious that no inspector for the Lamppost Painters' Union was on the job.) This magnanimous act of Pat's finished the job.

The question is, which man painted the greater number of lampposts — and how many more did he paint than the other? It isn't quite so obvious as it sounds.

No. 23   Average Speeds

We started on a motor trip the other day. On the journey to our destination we made as good time as was possible, but found on our arrival that we had averaged only ten miles an hour. (It was a lovely Sunday afternoon on one of America's finest superhighways, which explains this terrific speed.) Coming back that night over the same route, we found that traffic was lighter, so we were able to average fifteen miles an hour for the return journey, which you will admit is going places.

However, that's not the point. The point is — what was our average speed for the whole trip? We may warn you not to jump too hastily to conclusions or you may find yourself wrong.

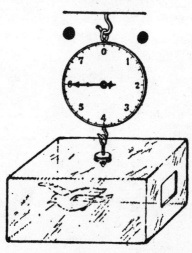

Our illustration shows a remarkable piece of apparatus invented by Professor I. Rackabrane. It is composed, as you see, of a glass box which is hung by a chain from a spring balance. The box weighs exactly six pounds. You will observe that there is a hole at one end of the box, and during the professor's absence a bird has made its way into the box and is flying about without touching the sides or the bottom in any way. We may state that this bird weighs exactly one pound.

Our artist has drawn the spring balance registering six pounds — the weight of the professor's glass box. We would like to know whether or not he is right. Would the entrance of a one-pound bird into such a box affect the weight of the box? Remember that the bird keeps flying and never touches the box in any way.

No. 25   A "New Deal" in Banking

A man went into a bank and cashed a check. There's nothing remarkable about that—but the teller, who was in a hurry, reversed the dollars and cents: That is, he gave the man as many dollars as there were cents in the check, and as many cents as there were dollars.

The man, who had no other money in his pocket, went out and spent $3.50. Then he counted his money and found that he still had exactly twice the value of the original check.

Now, assuming that a bank would really give you more money than you asked for (this is a puzzle, remember, and anything can happen in a puzzle), what was the value of the original check?

No. 26　　Mixed Doubles

Four men and their wives happened to be week-ending at a hotel which boasted two tennis courts. They were making a three-day stay, and as all were enthusiastic players, they arranged a tournament of mixed doubles. One match per day was to be played on each court — a man and a lady always playing against a man and a lady —and they managed matters so that no person ever played twice either with or against any other person.

If you had been on the committee arranging these six matches, could you have arrived at such a result? This puzzle may have a practical value if you should ever find yourself required to make a similar arrangement for tennis, bridge, or any partnership game.

```
L B ) R L N A C ( E U I
      R P N
      ─────
        P N A
        E L N
        ─────
          U A C
          U B B
          ─────
            U P
```

The letters above represent the figures in a sum in long division. All the figures, 1, 2, 3, 4, 5, 6, 7, 8, 9, and 0, are represented. When you have worked out the value of each letter and placed them in numerical order, beginning with 1 and ending with 0, they will spell a ten-letter word. To find the values of the letters, use the clues in the division. For instance, in the first subtraction we see that N from N gives N; N must therefore be zero. And as in the first multiplication E times B gives something ending in zero, either B or E must be 5, for 5 is the only figure which when multiplied by another figure will give something ending in zero. But later on we see that U times B also gives something ending in zero; therefore B must be 5, not E. And since E and U times B gives the zero result, both E and U must be even numbers. But we won't spoil the fun — work out the rest yourself.

No. 28   A Question of Current Rate

This puzzle has a way of creating confusion—just why, I don't know. It is entirely simple, and yet—

Well . . . here it is:

A man is in a boat in the middle of a stream. He drops a piece of wood overboard, and at once starts rowing upstream at a constant rate. He rows for ten minutes, then turns and rows downstream at the same rate, and catches the piece of wood three miles below the point at which he dropped it into the water. What was the rate of flow of the stream?

In order to avoid any confusion: The man loses no time in turning the boat nor does the difficulty of acquiring speed from a standing start bother him. Also we can ignore the possibility that he was drifting downstream when he dropped the piece of wood. He is assumed to be motionless at that instant.

1. Make a good English word out of the letters in

ROAST MULES

No letter is to be used oftener than it appears, and all letters are to be used. Just one word, obviously containing ten letters.

2. Work out the following sum in addition, substituting figures for the letters, so that it works out properly:

$$
\begin{array}{r}
S\ E\ N\ D \\
M\ O\ R\ E \\
\hline
M\ O\ N\ E\ Y
\end{array}
$$

That is, assign such values to the letters that E plus D equals Y, R plus N equals E (with or without anything to carry), and so on.

No. 30   Poker and Cigarettes

Here's a puzzle for which I am indebted to Charles E. Taylor of Fanwood, New Jersey.

Five men—let's call them Brown, Jones, Perkins, Riley, and Turner—are engaged in the national pastime of poker. They bring their cigarettes with them—Camels, Chesterfields, Lucky Strikes, Old Golds, and Raleighs—in these quantities: 20, 15, 8, 6, and 3, but not respectively in any case. The last hand has been dealt.

1. Perkins asked for three cards.

2. Riley has smoked half his cigarettes, or one less than Turner.

3. The man who smokes Chesterfields had originally as many more, half as many more, and 2½ more cigarettes than he has now.

4. The man who is drawing to an inside straight absent-mindedly lights the tipped end of his fifth cigarette.

5. The man who smokes Lucky Strikes has smoked two more than anyone else, including Perkins.

6. On the deal just completed Brown receives as many aces as he originally had cigarettes.

7. No one has smoked all his cigarettes.

8. The man who smokes Camels asks Jones to pass Brown's matches.

Now from the above facts and figures — can you figure out which man brought which brand of cigarettes, and how many?

A man went into a store and bought goods to the extent of thirty-four cents. The only money he had was a dollar, a three-cent piece, and a two-cent piece. The tradesman had only a half-dollar and a quarter. But at this moment a stranger turned up with two dimes, a nickel, a two-cent piece, and a cent. The result was that correct change was given and everybody was happy, though, oddly enough, nobody got any of his own coins back. How did they make change?

ANSWERS TO DETECTOGRAMS

No. 1 So This Is London!

The professor said the fog was so thick he couldn't see two feet ahead—yet he knew when he came to the middle of a block!

No. 2 They Usually Forget Something

The note, although misspelled, poorly expressed, and written by a seemingly illiterate hand, was punctuated properly in two places. A semicolon and a comma would not have been used had the writer been as ignorant as the rest of his letter indicated. Force of habit had betrayed him.

No. 3 An Easy Combination

It would have been impossible for Fellows to have hastily dialed a number in the dark. Try it!

No. 4 Too Clever

The professor knew someone had been in the room after the message had been scrawled because the pen with which it was written was found in the pen tray. Dawson died before he finished the message, therefore he could not have placed it there himself.

No. 5   The Ex-Wife Murder

Rogers could not have known that his ex-wife had been shot unless he had guilty knowledge of the crime. The maid did not say why she had been taken to the hospital. Yet Rogers' first words on entering the hospital were, "Who shot her?"

No. 6   A Rum Regatta

Starritt whispered to each, "Run the other man's boat." As the owner of the last boat to reach Miami was to get the money, each one naturally raced the boat he was driving. By doing so, he hoped to beat his own boat, which was being driven by one of the others.

No. 7   Shadowed

There was only one man trailing Jim Wilson at a time. His brother Bill merely hid near the hotel until he saw Jim leave, with the detective following, and then walked in and waited for Jim to return. When he wanted to leave, his brother Jim would take a walk, with the detective following, and then Bill would return to his hideout.

No. 8   A Question of Identity

As Diana Lane was walking down the corridor with her back to Nora, it was impossible for the servant to know whether or not Diana was wearing her famous emerald pendant.

No. 9   A Yachtsman's Alibi

As Picus said there was no breeze, the distress flag would have hung limp against the mast, and the captain could not have told whether or not the flag was upside down.

No. 10   Murder at Coney Island

Jasper said he found the woman sitting up in the middle of the chariot. The doctor said she had died instantly. The motion of the merry-go-round would have made it impossible for a dead body to remain upright in the middle of the chariot. It would have slumped over before Jasper touched it.

No. 11

PROFESSOR STABUS STIGGINS, ILL.
CERTAINLY ROBBERY WAS FAKED STOP
CHADWICK SLIPPED BADLY WHEN HE SAID
HE SAW MAN CLIMB LADDER OPEN WINDOW
AND ENTER HIS BEDROOM STOP AS YOU
FOUND LADDER HOOKED TO INSIDE SILL
THIS WOULD HAVE BEEN IMPOSSIBLE STOP
HOLD CHADWICK FOR INVESTIGATION

                        E F CAVANAUGH

No. 12

PROFESSOR STABUS STIGGINS, PA.
NURSE CLAIMS MADAM UNDRESSED SELF
STOP YOU FOUND MADAMS DRESS ON TOP
OF PILE OF CLOTHES STOP HAVE NO DOUBT

THIS CLUE WILL LEAD YOU TO ULTIMATE
SOLUTION OF TRAGEDY ANDREW J HUDOCK

No. 13
PROFESSOR STABUS STIGGINS, ARIZ.
GOT YOU STOP YOU AND JOE MOVED EITHER
ONE OR BOTH OF THE BOULDERS STOP
VERY CLEVER STIGGIE STOP AWAITING JOES
ARRIVAL   VIC

No. 14
PROFESSOR STABUS STIGGINS, OKLA.
AS STINSONS WOUND INSTANTLY FATAL
IMPOSSIBLE FOR HIM TO HAVE SHOT HIM-
SELF AND HAVE HEAD ON OUTSTRETCHED
ARMS STOP AM ARRIVING TOMORROW ON
PRIVATE INVESTIGATION HARRY BECKMAN

No. 15
PROFESSOR STABUS STIGGINS, CAL.
SUPPOSE YOU FOUND NO BUTTONS IN
CHARRED SUITING STOP WILL LEAVE PROS-
ECUTION TO YOU   PRESTON

No. 16
PROFESSOR STABUS STIGGINS, WASH. D. C.
TELEGRAM STATES JOHNSON JONES AND
JEFFRIES ARE THIEF BLACKMAILER AND
MURDERER BUT NOT RESPECTIVELY STOP
IF JONES THE BLACKMAILER JOHNSON AND
JEFFRIES ARE THIEF AND MURDERER BUT

NOT RESPECTIVELY THEREFORE ONLY POSSIBLE REARRANGEMENT OF NAMES IS IN RESPECTIVE ORDER AS FOLLOWS JEFFRIES JONES AND JOHNSON THIEF BLACKMAILER AND MURDERER STOP THUS JOHNSON THE MURDERER   KEELER

No. 17

PROFESSOR STABUS STIGGINS, N. Y.

HAVE JUDSON IN CUSTODY STOP HE WAS ONE COSTUMED AS ROBIN HOOD AND IS MYSTIFIED HOW YOU KNEW HE SAT NEXT DEAD WOMAN STOP AM SURE ANSWER VERY SIMPLE AND THAT IS BECAUSE OF CRUMBS ON CHAIR STOP ALL OTHERS SO COSTUMED AS TO MAKE IT IMPOSSIBLE FOR THEM TO HAVE LEFT CRUMBS ON CHAIR STOP NICE DEDUCING WHAT   MORAN

No. 18

As Black's laboratory door was found locked and bolted and no one could have left by windows, obviously Black committed suicide.

No. 19

Winton Loomis' story was impossible because, had he examined the three front rooms before going to the studio at the rear, he could not have made mud tracks near his wife's body, as there would have been no mud left on his shoes.

No. 20

As Wilterding had an unquestionable alibi and no one but the murderer knew the cause of death until after the autopsy, Wilterding was innocent and the murderer was the writer of the note.

No. 21

STABUS STIGGINS, N. Y.
YOU HAD ME GUESSING BUT IVE GOT IT STOP THE COOK IS A MAN   JOE KAVANAGH

No. 22

PROFESSOR STABUS STIGGINS, M. D.
MURDERERS GENERALLY SLIP STOP WATSONS MISTAKE WAS IN CLOSING WINDOW AFTER PUSHING ROGERS OUT STOP HAD ROGERS REALLY COMMITTED SUICIDE WICKERSHAM WOULD OF COURSE HAVE FOUND WINDOW OPEN STOP THANKS FOR COOPERATION   JOHN J FAHEY

No. 23

PROFESSOR STABUS STIGGINS, N. Y.
IF WOUND INSTANTLY FATAL AND SELF INFLICTED OWINGS COULD NOT POSSIBLY HAVE NOTE GRASPED IN HAND STOP HE WOULD HAVE DROPPED IT WITH PISTOL AT MOMENT OF DEATH STOP AS WIFE ADMITS BEING ALONE WITH HIM SHE OF COURSE IS MURDERESS   CALVIN GODDARD

No. 24
PROFESSOR STABUS STIGGINS, N. Y.
THANKS FOR REPORT ALLENS STORY OF
COURSE PREPOSTEROUS STOP HAD TRAG-
EDY OCCURRED AS HE CLAIMS GIRLS COAT
AND HAT WOULD NOT HAVE BEEN WASHED
ASHORE OPPOSITE POINT IN MIDDLE OF
RIVER WHERE CANOE CAPSIZED STOP HAVE
HIM HELD   TRACY STATES ATTORNEY

No. 25
PROFESSOR STABUS STIGGINS, K. A.
AS NEITHER HUDSON NOR RANDOLPH
EITHER KILLER OR LEADER AND AS BRON-
SON IS NOT LEADER AND WINTERS NOT
KILLER BRONSON IS KILLER AND WINTERS
IS LEADER   W C GORDON

No. 26
PROFESSOR STABUS STIGGINS, ILL.
UNDERSTAND WHY YOURE HOLDING RINK-
ER STOP HAD HIS STORY BEEN TRUE THERE
WOULD HAVE BEEN BLOOD ON BLUEPRINT
STOP THANKS   DOMIANUS

ANSWERS TO PUZZLES

No. 1   The Bookworm's Journey
The bookworm traveled only three and a half
inches in going from the first page of Volume I

to the last page of Volume III! When three books are stood together, the first page of Volume I is on the right and the last page of Volume III is on the left. The worm, starting from the first page of Volume I, went through two covers, the paper in Volume II, and through two more covers, which brought him to the last page of Volume III—this would be a total of three and a half inches.

No. 2   A One-Word Puzzle

The letters O R E D W N O form—ONE WORD!

Now, lest you feel this one tricky, the letters A B E N O T Y form the word BAYONET. The difficulty in this last one is that few people think of -ET as a word ending.

No. 3   The Fly and the Bicycles

The fly flew exactly 15 miles. How come? Well, the cyclists rode toward each other over a twenty-mile stretch at a constant speed of ten miles per hour, until their front wheels touched. Clearly, then, they rode for exactly an hour. The fly started to fly back and forth when they started, and flew till they met, at a constant speed of fifteen miles per hour—that is, he flew for one hour at fifteen miles per hour—so he flew fifteen miles. That's all.

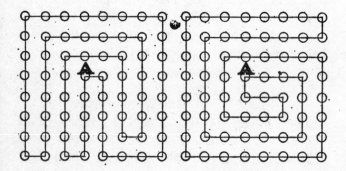

Above are shown two routes by which all the towns may be visited once, and only once, returning to the starting place, in only sixteen straight trips. These are the only possible solutions with so few moves. Most people can't do the trick in less than seventeen.

No. 5   Word Enigma Puzzle
"The quality of mercy is not strained; it droppeth as the gentle rain from heaven."

No. 6   The Sliding Letters Puzzle

INAdequate	fascINAtor
fINAnciers	coordINAte
chINAberry	unorigINAl
nomINAtors	concertINA

No. 7   Letter-Addition Puzzle

I	RETAIN
IT	CERTAIN
TIE	REACTION
RITE (or TIRE)	CREMATION
INTER	IMPORTANCE

No. 8   Wine and Water

The question was, did the man take more wine from the wine bottle than water from the water bottle, or the other way around, or — That "or —" was the key to the business. As a matter of fact the same quantity of wine was transferred from the wine bottle as water from the water bottle.

Let's say that the glass held a quarter of a pint. There was a pint of wine and a pint of water. Now, after the first manipulation, the wine bottle contained three quarters of a pint of wine, and the water bottle one pint of water mixed with a quarter of a pint of wine—five quarters of a pint of liquid. Now, the second manipulation consisted of taking away one fifth of the contents of the water bottle—that is, one fifth of a pint of water mixed with one fifth of a quarter of a pint of wine. We thus leave behind in the water bottle four fifths of a quarter of a pint of wine—that is to say, one fifth of a pint—and transfer the same amount of water to the wine bottle.

No. 9 Links and Links

A little rule which may be handy to remember is that the length of a chain of similar circular links is equal to the inner width of the ring, or link, multiplied by the number of links and added to twice the thickness of the metal in the ring.

Now, it is said that Brown captured six more rings than Jones and that Brown's chain was sixteen inches long, while Jones' was six inches long. The temptation is to assume that a chain of six links is ten inches long. But if you look at the accompanying drawing you will see that the

difference in length of the chains is not six full links, but five links plus the inner width minus twice the thickness of the iron.

Applying our rule to a chain of five links, we get five times the inner width plus twice the thickness of the iron (one inch). We then add the inner width minus twice the thickness of the iron (one inch again), which gives us simply six times the inner width as the difference in length of the two chains. We are told that this is ten inches, therefore the inner width must have been one sixth of ten, or one and two thirds.

Knowing the inner width, we now apply it first to a chain sixteen inches long and then to a chain six inches long, which gives us nine links and three links respectively—with each one.

No. 10   Ringing the Changes
PADRES, SPARED, SPADER, RASPED, PARSED, REPADS, SPREAD, DRAPES.

No. 11   The Flock of Ducks
There must have been 101 ducks in that flock. He sold half the flock and half a duck over (50½ plus ½, or 51), leaving 50; then he sold a third of these and a third of a duck (16⅔ plus ⅓, or 17), leaving 33; then he sold a quarter of these and three quarters of a duck (8¼ plus ¾, or 9), leaving 24; then he sold a fifth of these and a fifth of a duck (4⅘ plus ⅕, or 5), which left 19 he could not sell.

No. 12   A Matter of Cutting Cheese
A cheese may be cut into fifteen pieces in four straight cuts. It is a question of making sure that each cut intersects every other cut, and that no

two intersections shall coincide. The real difficulty is in "seeing" the result of the cuts. Without actually sitting down and cutting a cheese we do not believe that it is possible for the mind to visualize the effect of more than four cuts—and it isn't easy with four.

No. 13   A Puzzle by Candlelight

Those candles must have burned for three and three-quarter hours. At the end of that time the four-hour candle had one sixteenth of its length left, and the five-hour candle had four sixteenths.

No. 14   Election Day Puzzle

All you have to do is to add the sum of the three pluralities (268) to the total of votes cast (1,648), giving 1,916, and then divide by 4, which gives 479, which is the number of votes received by Mr. Smith, the winner. After that, simple subtraction will give the votes received by the other three—471 by Brown, 403 by Robinson, and 295 by Detwiler.

As for the other definition question, a plurality is the margin over the remainder of the total votes cast. If, say, there are 1,000 votes cast and A receives 600, B 300, and C 100, A is elected by a plurality of 300 over B and 500 over C; his majority is 200, the difference between his 600 and the 400 received by the other candidates. In usual practice the plurality over C would not be mentioned, the plurality over the nearest rival being the only one stated.

No. 15   Stolen Treasure Puzzle

The best answer requires eleven manipulations, which may be tabulated as follows:

1. Treasure down.
2. Boy down—treasure up.
3. Youth down—boy up.
4. Treasure down.
5. Man down—youth and treasure up.
6. Treasure down.
7. Boy down—treasure up.
8. Treasure down.
9. Youth down—boy up.
10. Boy down—treasure up.
11. Treasure down.

No. 16   Par Golf

The best two distances are 125 yards and 100 yards. These will get you out in 26 strokes. The catch—if you can call it a catch—is the fact that you must play No. 5—275 yards—in three 125-yard shots and one backward 100-yard shot. Otherwise it is impossible to play that hole using the two distances. Under the conditions such a backward shot is perfectly allowable.

No. 17   A Little Pure Reason

The plane bound eastward would crash. The earth revolves from west to east, and this revolution would add to the flying time of the east-bound plane and subtract from the other.

Call the three men A, B, and C, and say that C was unmarked. The smarter man—let us say A—would say to himself: "I am laughing at B, because B has a smudged face; C may also be laughing at B; but B is laughing too, and not at C, for C's face is clean. Therefore B must be laughing at me—my face must be dirty.

No. 18   The Captive Princess
The knight left at twelve noon and rode twelve miles per hour. The distance was sixty miles.

No. 19   Nine Tricky Dots

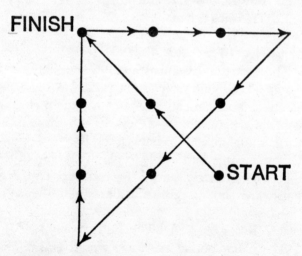

Solution above shows how to draw a line

through every one of the dots, making only three turnings. We never said you couldn't go outside the diagram!

No. 20   A New Match Puzzle

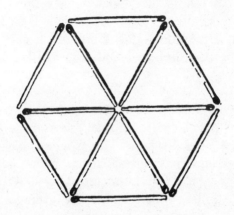

Arrange the matches as shown here and you will have six pens all of the same size, enclosed by twelve matches.

No. 21   Airplane Racing

There were thirteen planes in that race. You see, as it was around a circular course there were just as many planes in front of Jimmy Tailspin as there were behind him! A third of the number of planes in the race minus one — Jimmy's — plus three quarters of the number of planes in the race minus one gives you the number of planes.

Thirteen is the only number that will satisfy those conditions.

No. 22   Painting the Lampposts

Pat must have painted six more lampposts than Mike, no matter how many posts there were. Suppose twelve on each side: then Pat painted fifteen; Mike, nine. If a hundred on each side, Pat painted a hundred and three; Mike, ninety-seven.

No. 23   Average Speeds

Most people will say that the average speed was 12½ miles per hour. This is wrong. Take any distance, say sixty miles. This would require six hours going and four hours returning — ten hours for 120 miles, which makes the average speed 12 miles per hour. No matter what distance you select, the answer will be the same.

No. 24   Try This One When You Want an Argument

Our artist is wrong. The spring balance should register seven pounds. The weight of the bird, even though it is not touching the box, must be added to it. When a bird flies, its weight is supported on columns on air under its wings and body, and the pressure on these columns is transferred to whatever the air may be resting on — in this case the bottom of the box.

No. 25   A "New Deal" in Banking

The original check was for $14.32. Reverse
these figures and you get $32.14, from which if
you subtract $3.50, the result will be $28.64,
which is double $14.32. Where most people slip is
here: They realize that the number of cents in the
original check must be twice the number of
dollars plus 3, but they forget that a 1 must be
carried to complete the subtraction of the $3.50
so that the number of cents must be twice the
number of dollars plus 3 plus 1.

No. 26   Mixed Doubles

Call the men A, B, D, E, and their wives a,
b, d, e. Then they may play as follows:

First Court

1st day—A and d vs. B and e

2nd day—A and e vs. D and b

3rd day—A and b vs. E and d

Second Court

D and a vs. E and b

E and a vs. B and d

B and a vs. D and e

Not only are the conditions fulfilled, but no
man ever plays with or against his own wife—an
ideal arrangement, you will agree.

No. 27   Letter-Division Puzzle

1 2 3 4 5 6 7 8 9 0

R E P U B L I C A N

No. 28   A Question of Current Rate

The rate of flow of the stream was three miles in twenty minutes, or nine miles an hour. The man rowed upstream for ten minutes, then downstream at the same rate till he caught the piece of wood. When he went upstream the current hindered him; when he went downstream it helped him in the same proportion. Therefore it took him another ten minutes to catch his piece of wood, or twenty minutes in all, during which the wood had drifted three miles. It doesn't matter in the least how fast or how slowly the man rowed.

No. 29   Two Word Puzzles

From ROAST MULES you can make the word SOMERSAULT.

As for SEND MORE MONEY, the values are as follows:

1	2	3	4	5	6	7	8	9	0
M	Y			E	N	D	R	S	O

Obviously you saw that all the digits were not represented and that M was 1. Now if M (1) plus S gave a result in two figures, S had to be 8 or 9; and, no matter which it was, O had to be zero. But the previous addition was O (zero) plus E, which could never have 1 to carry in its result; therefore S was 9 and not 8. With these three values assigned, it was obvious that N was one more than E. Zero plus E gave N, so there must have been 1 to carry from the addition before. And in that same previous addition R plus N gave E. Now 9 plus anything results in the same thing less 1 (9 plus 8 equals 17, in which you put down 7 and carry 1, and 7 is 1 less than 8), but we have already determined that S is 9. Then R has to be 8, and 1 is carried from the first addition. A few trials will show that 5 and 6 are the only values that will satisfy E and N—and the problem is solved.

No. 30   Poker and Cigarettes

Here is the logical way of getting at the answer: Take the facts in order and see what each reveals, then combine the information.

From fact 1 we see that Perkins is not the man mentioned in fact 4.

From fact 2 we see that Riley had an even number of cigarettes.

From fact 3 we see that the man who smoked Chesterfields had originally 15, and has smoked 10 (15 is the only one of the numbers given that will fit this statement).

From fact 4 we see that this man smokes Raleighs. (Raleighs are supplied with tips; none of the other brands mentioned is.) We also see that he is not Perkins (No. 1 above), nor Brown (No. 6 below).

From fact 5 we see that the man who smokes Luckies has smoked at least 12 (see No. 3) and that he is not Perkins. Also he cannot be Riley, for 12 is more than half of any of the numbers; nor can he be Turner, for 12 is more than half of any of the numbers, plus 1 (No. 2). The only numbers that can apply to Lucky Strikes are 15 and 20; we know that there were 15 Chesterfields, so there must have been 20 Luckies originally. He is not Brown (No. 6). Therefore he is Jones.

From fact 6 we see that Brown had only 3 cigarettes originally.

From fact 8 we see that the man who smokes Camels is neither Jones nor Brown.

Now we can make a table:

Number	Brand	Smoker
20	Luckies	Jones
15	Chesterfields	
8		
6		
3		Brown

With this before us, we proceed: Brown had only 3 cigarettes. Therefore he did not smoke Luckies (20) or Chesterfields (15) or Raleighs (at least 5). From No. 7 we see that he does not smoke Camels; therefore his is the only remaining brand—Old Gold. Now we know that the man who smokes Raleighs is neither Perkins nor Brown (No. 4), nor is he Jones, for we have settled that Jones smokes Luckies. He must therefore be either Riley or Turner. Whichever he may be, the remaining man has a choice of either Chesterfields or Camels. But look at No. 2: "Riley has smoked half his cigarettes, or one less than Turner." Ten, the number of Chesterfields consumed, will not fit this statement. Therefore whoever smokes Raleighs, Riley or Turner, the other smokes Camels, which leaves only one man, Perkins, to be the Chesterfield smoker. Our table now looks like this:

Number	Brand	Smoker
20	Luckies	Jones
15	Chesterfields	Perkins
8		
6		
3	Old Golds	Brown

Riley, Turner, Raleighs, and Camels remain to annoy us. Well, see facts 2 and 4. Whoever smokes Raleighs has smoked 5. He lighted the tipped end, but it is definitely stated that it was his fifth cigarette. And Riley has smoked half his cigarettes, or one less than Turner. Five is not half of either 8 or 6; but 4 is half of 8 and is one less than 5; therefore Riley had the 8 and they were not Raleighs. They must have been Camels — and that's that.

No. 31   A Matter of Change

The best way to solve the problem is this: Let everyone put down on the counter the coins he has, and let us represent them by the number of cents in each:

Customer: 100, 3, 2. Tradesman: 50, 25. Stranger: 10, 10, 5, 2, 1.

Now, remembering that the purchase cost 34 cents, it is plain that the tradesman has to receive 109 cents (his 75 cents plus the 34 cents the customer owes him); the customer, 71 cents; and the stranger, his 28 cents. The rest is a matter of arrangement, remembering that nobody got back any of his original coins. The tradesman takes 100, 5, 2, and 2; the customer 50, 10, 10, and 1; and the stranger the remaining two coins, 25 and 3.